J 973.04 CUNN

MAR 2010

W9-BFD-704

Canadian Americans

SPIRIT
of America®

Canadian AMERICANS

By Kevin Cunningham

*Content Adviser: Joel Wurl, Curator and Assistant Director, Immigration
History Research Center, University of Minnesota,
Minneapolis, Minnesota*

The
**Child's
World**

The Child's World®
Chanhassen, Minnesota

Norfolk Public Library
139 Main Street
Norfolk, MA 02056

7

Canadian AMERICANS

Published in the United States of America by The Child's World®
P.O. Box 326 • Chanhassen, MN 55317-0326 • 800-599-READ • www.childsworld.com

Acknowledgments
The Child's World®: Mary Berendes, Publishing Director

Editorial Directions, Inc.: E. Russell Primm, Editorial Director; Pam Rosenberg, Line Editor; Katie Marsico, Assistant Editor; Matthew Messbarger, Editorial Assistant; Susan Hindman, Copy Editor; Susan Ashley, Proofreader; Julie Zaveloff, Chris Simms, and Peter Garnham, Fact Checkers; Tim Griffin/IndexServ, Indexer; Dawn Friedman, Photo Researcher; Linda S. Koutris, Photo Selector

The Design Lab: Kathleen Petelinsek, Art Direction; Kari Thornborough, Page Production

Photos
Cover/frontispiece: John D. Soper family, Soper Post Office, North Dakota, circa 1896 or 1897

Cover photographs ©: North Dakota Institute for Regional Studies, North Dakota State University/Fred Hultsrand Collection; Ron Watts/Corbis.

Interior photographs ©: AP/Wide World: 6 (Bill Sikes), 27 (Jim Rogash); Bettmann/Corbis: 10, 13, 15, 28; Corbis: 7 (Leonard de Selva), 8, 9 (Hulton-Deutsch Collection), 12 (Historical Picture Archive), 17, 23 (Steve Chenn), 24 (Ron Watts), 25 (William Taufic); Getty Images/Image Bank/Jeremy Woodhouse: 20; Magnum Photos/Jean Gaumy: 22; North Dakota Institute for Regional Studies, North Dakota State University/Fred Hulstrand Collection: 11; Philip Gould/Corbis: 18, 19.

Registration
The Child's World®, Spirit of America®, and their associated logos are the sole property and registered trademarks of The Child's World®.

Copyright ©2004 by The Child's World®. All rights reserved. No part of this book may be reproduced or utilized in any form or by any means without written permission from the publisher.

Library of Congress Cataloging-in-Publication Data
Cunningham, Kevin.
  Canadian Americans / by Kevin Cunningham.
    v. cm.—(Our cultural heritage)
  Includes index.
  Contents : The Canadian Americans—The Cajuns—Canadians in the United States—Canadian-American contributions.
  ISBN 1-59296-178-9 (lib. bdg. : alk. paper)
  1. Canadian Americans—Juvenile literature. [1. Canadian Americans.] I. Title. II. Series. E184.C2 C68 2004
  973'.0411—dc22   2003018092

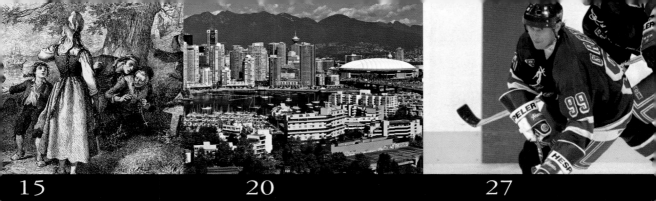

Contents

Chapter ONE

The Canadian Americans

Interesting Fact

▸ The border between Canada and the United States, from the Atlantic Ocean to the Pacific Ocean, is 3,987 miles (6,416 kilometers) long.

THE BORDER BETWEEN CANADA AND THE UNITED States is the world's longest undefended national border. Although the United States has 11 times as many people, Canada is slightly bigger than the United States in size. In fact, Canada is the second-largest country in the world—nearly as large as all of Europe.

Niagara Falls straddles the border between Canada and the United States. Each year, more than 12 million visitors view this 12,000-year-old river on the Canadian side of the falls in the province of Ontario and also on the American side in the state of New York.

Prescott Gate, built in 1797, was one of six entrance gates to the old city of Quebec.

The two countries are close friends now, but things were different before Canada became independent. Back then, Great Britain controlled Canada's government. After the American Revolution, the British and Americans were not on friendly terms. It took until the 1840s for them to agree to a final border between the United States and Canada. When Britain allowed Canada to govern itself after 1867, the United States and its northern neighbor became closer.

Canadian **immigrants** have been coming to the United States almost since the day the Revolutionary War ended. In the 1790s, Canadians, especially French Canadians, stampeded into the New England states of New York, Vermont, New Hampshire, and Maine in search of cheap land.

Immigrants continued to arrive for more than 100 years. Most were from Quebec, a **province**

Interesting Fact

▶ Almost half of the people from Maine have Canadian ancestors.

Interesting Fact

▶ The first permanent settlement in the city of Detroit, Michigan, was founded by a group of French Canadians led by Antoine de Lamothe Cadillac on July 24, 1701. There is a statue of Cadillac and a historical marker honoring this group in Hart Plaza in Detroit.

where people spoke French instead of English. From 1840 to 1930, more than 900,000 French Canadians came to the United States. Half of them stayed for good.

Many were poor farmers who needed jobs. Factory jobs in the United States paid more money than farming did. French-speaking immigrants headed for factories in towns such as Lowell, Massachusetts; Troy, New York; and Manchester, New Hampshire. They set up neighborhoods called *petits Canadas*—French for "little Canadas." French traditions, such as practicing the Roman Catholic religion, took root. Other French Canadians followed, happy to settle among people like themselves.

Not everyone went to the cities though. Farmers went to Maine, hoping to take advantage

Most Canadian immigrants did not move to large American cities. They decided to call smaller towns, such as Lowell, Massachusetts, home instead. Lowell's factories and mills needed workers and Canadian immigrants were ready to work.

of warmer weather and more sun. In about 1850, logging took off in the woods of northern New York and other nearby states. French-Canadian lumberjacks showed up to work with everything they owned on their backs. Canadian areas in the west grew, too. When farmland became scarce in Canada, immigrants from both the English and French parts of the country came to the United States looking for cheap land. Many of them settled in Illinois, Minnesota, and Michigan, among other places.

Railroads between cities in Quebec and New England made the trip south easier and cheaper. Around 450,000 Canadians immigrants arrived between 1880 and 1890. One out of every three came from Quebec, the rest from the other provinces. It's important to note many of these "Canadians" were

Trains like this one provided passenger service between Montreal and cities such as Boston. This service started in 1851. Trains such as "The Red Wing" were used for overnight trips and "The Alouette" handled the daytime trips. The names of these two trains were the English and French language names for the red-winged blackbird common to Montreal.

born in Europe, particularly in Ireland, Germany, and Scandinavia. They only meant to stop over in Canada. Once they earned a little money, they moved on to the United States. Immigrants today do the same thing, but more often come from Asian countries such as China.

Immigration from Canada began to slow down in the 1930s. The United States and much of the world were suffering through the Great Depression. Job opportunities in the United States became scarce, and few people wanted to take the chance of leaving Canada and not finding work.

At the height of the Great Depression in 1933, more than 11 million people were unemployed. That was about 25 percent of America's entire work force.

Today, millions of Americans claim Canadian **ancestors.** Because most Canadian immigrants were too poor to travel far, Canadian Americans today tend to live in the north. Those with English-speaking ancestors are often found in New York, Michigan, Wisconsin, Minnesota, and North Dakota. In recent years, though, Canadian senior citizens have also settled in warm places such as Florida and Arizona, while younger workers seem to prefer California. About 11 million Americans have French-speaking ancestors. About three million of these are French Canadian. Most live in New York, Vermont, New Hampshire, and Maine. The one exception is the Cajun people of southern Louisiana.

Interesting Fact

▶ Louisiana is not the only place where Acadians settled. The National Park Service maintains a Maine Acadian Culture site. It is located in Madawaska, Maine, in the St. John Valley. Most of Madawaska's nearly 5,000 residents are of Acadian descent and speak French. Each year, the town holds an Acadian Festival.

This modest house shared by these Canadian immigrants was typical of the homes of its time. It would not have been very comfortable to live in.

BEFORE EUROPEANS ARRIVED, NATIVE CANADIAN TRIBES—CALLED FIRST Nations in Canada—lived throughout North America. Different tribes had different lifestyles. Prairie peoples, such as the Assiniboine and Cree, hunted bison and other prairie animals and also fished for sturgeon. The Huron, of what is now Ontario, farmed and traded. The Inuit peoples of the far north lived by a combination of fishing and hunting sea mammals such as whales and seals.

Samuel de Champlain opened up North America for the Europeans. He helped found Canada's first permanent European towns. Located on the Atlantic Coast, these towns became part of a colony the French named Acadia. The British soon followed. Unfortunately for the First Nations, the Europeans brought diseases such as smallpox. The people of the First Nations couldn't fight off these new germs. Many Native Canadians died, and whole tribes disappeared forever.

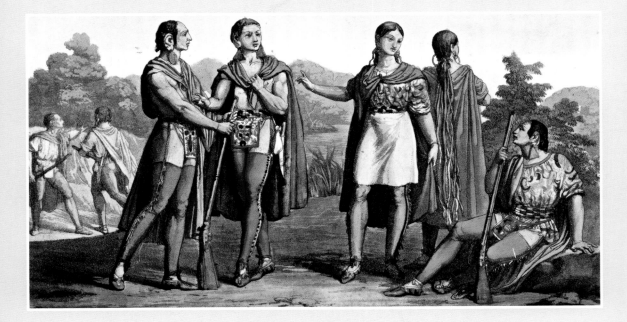

The British and the French began to explore—and fight over—Canada. British fur trappers traveled into the area around Hudson Bay. At the same time, the French explored to the south. Louis Joliet and Jacques Marquette, using canoes, explored the Mississippi River as far south as modern Arkansas. Frenchman René-Robert Cavelier, Sieur de La Salle, journeyed around the Great Lakes region and on the Illinois River. Then, in 1682, he traveled down the Mississippi to the Gulf of Mexico.

All three men have cities named after them. In fact, dozens of American towns and cities, such as St. Louis, Detroit, and Louisville, owe their names to the French.

Chapter Two

The Cajuns

Interesting Fact

▶ Years of fighting smallpox by vaccinating people around the world allowed health professionals to wipe out the dangerous disease. The last natural case of smallpox in the world was recorded in Somalia in 1977. In 1979, the World Health Organization announced that the disease had been wiped out.

LOUISIANA'S CAJUNS NUMBER MORE THAN ONE million people. Once considered mysterious because they lived on the hard-to-reach **bayou,** Cajuns today are important as fishers, farmers, and oil workers. But there's a sad story behind their journey to America.

The word *Cajun* is a shortened version of *Acadian.* After fighting the French for one hundred years, the British took over Acadia in 1713. They renamed it Nova Scotia and told the Acadians to swear to be loyal to the British king. But the Acadians refused to be ruled by Britain.

They were still refusing in 1753, when a British officer named Charles Lawrence took charge. Lawrence was determined to drive off the Acadians. Acting in secret, he brought in soldiers to arrest them and ships to carry them away. The following year, when both were in place, the **expulsion** began.

The British burned down the Acadians' homes and threw them onto the ships. Once on board, the

Acadians were taken south. Hundreds died of cold or smallpox. Sometimes families became separated. When ships docked in Massachusetts or Connecticut, Acadians under age 21 were sometimes forced to work for American landowners. Those unlucky enough to dock in South Carolina became slaves. The British dropped more Acadians on the coast of France.

One group, however, ended up in France's Caribbean colonies. After being mistreated there, these Acadians moved to Louisiana, a French territory at the mouth of the Mississippi River.

Thousands of Acadians were deported to New England, the Southern colonies, or to Europe (England and France). The Acadians were allowed to return to Nova Scotia in 1764, but by that time their land was occupied by other settlers.

The country of Spain paid for more than 1,600 Acadians from France to travel to Louisiana in 1785. In 1762, the French had granted control of Louisiana to Spain. The Spanish were anxious to get people to settle in Louisiana to help keep the English from trying to take over their territory. The Spanish government said it would pay a commission to anyone who could provide settlers. Henri Peyroux de la Coudreniere saw this as an opportunity to make money. He convinced many Acadians in France to sail to Louisiana and make it their home.

After the cold and damp of Canada, the Acadians had to adjust to Louisiana's swamps. But adjust they did. They drained water from the farmland and enjoyed rich fishing in the Mississippi River and the Gulf of Mexico. Native Americans taught them to grow new crops and catch new kinds of fish.

Acadians living in France, Quebec, and other parts of the United States soon arrived to join their relatives and friends. In 1785, a New Orleans man named Henri Peyroux de la Coudreniere led 1,624 Acadians back from France. Escaped Caribbean slaves and other immigrants joined the Acadians. Somewhere along the line, they shortened their name to Cajuns.

The French sold the Louisiana Territory to the United States in 1803. Nine years later, its southern area, the Territory of Orleans, became Louisiana, the 18th state. That marked the start of an up-and-down century for the Cajuns. As sugar became a popular crop, rich growers acquired the best land. Small Cajun farms couldn't keep up. The year 1901 brought a much bigger change—the discovery of oil. While the oil industry provided jobs, it also damaged Louisiana's **environment.** New waterways for ships altered the bayou. Both affected the Cajuns' hunting, farming, trapping, and fishing.

Throughout the 20th century, Cajuns fought to save their **culture.** On the one hand, books

"A BURNIC GUSHER"
Photo By Parnett Bros.
Neg. #2.   LAKE CHARLES
LA

Industry has had both good and bad effects on society. The oil industry created many jobs in Louisiana but it also hurt the environment. Oil fires like this one can do lots of damage. It sometimes takes a long time to put out the fires and the pollutants in the thick, black smoke can hurt fragile ecosystems.

about Cajuns were published for the first time. On the other, speaking French in public schools became illegal in 1922. The last French-language newspaper went out of business in 1955.

Cajun music is meant for dancing. Dances like the one-step, two-step and waltzes are traditional Cajun dances. Dancing ("Fais-do-do" in Cajun) was once the major social activity in Cajun society. The most important musical instrument in Cajun music is the diatonic accordion.

In recent years, though, Cajun culture has earned new respect. A government organization, the Council for the Development of French in Louisiana (CODOFIL), began to teach French in schools again. Professors recorded Cajun folk tales and music for the first time. Cajun food became popular in places far from the bayou. After 400 years of trouble, the Cajuns had a home at last.

LOUISIANA SCHOOLS BEGAN TO TEACH FRENCH AGAIN IN THE 1970S. BUT IT WAS Standard French, the same language you would hear in Paris. Cajuns said this ignored their way of life. Cajuns use a **patois** that mixes French with words and ideas from English, Spanish, German, Portuguese, and several African and Native American languages.

The Cajun language split from standard French when the Acadians left Canada.

The same thing happened to Quebec's French speakers. Today, their kind of French, called Quebecois (kay-bah-KWA), can confuse visitors from France. The people in each place borrowed words from those around them. That is one of the ways languages grow and change.

To add to the confusion, the Cajun patois still includes words from the 17th and 18th centuries. No one else uses these words anymore except Cajuns. The Cajuns also shorten standard French words, the way they turned *Acadian* into *Cajun.* They do the same thing to phrases. As a result, a person from France has even more trouble understanding Cajun than they do understanding Quebecois. Yet all are considered French languages.

At first, the CODOFIL program refused to teach Cajun. They said it wasn't proper French. Today, though, CODOFIL lets Louisianans learn both standard French and Cajun by holding classes, special programs, and events. It also acts to correct media mistakes about the Cajun people and culture.

Chapter THREE

Canadians in the United States

Vancouver (below) is the third largest city in Canada (after Toronto and Montreal). It is the leading Pacific Coast seaport and the industrial, cultural, and financial center of British Columbia.

ACCORDING TO THE UNITED NATIONS, CANADA IS one of the best countries to live in. It has a stable government, good schools, and guaranteed health care. It trades with rich partners such as the United States and China. Most of its nearly 31 million citizens live so near the border they can watch American television or shop in American stores.

Yet since 1970, more than 600,000 Canadian immigrants have entered the United States. While some worked for a time and then returned home, thousands stayed. Why? To find an answer, it helps to understand the differences between most immigrant groups and Canadians.

Today, immigrants from poorer countries face many of the problems that Canadians, especially French Canadians, dealt with one hundred years ago. They don't speak English. They often settle in poor areas—"little Somalias" or "little Koreas"—with others from their home countries. Sometimes a father and his sons or brothers come first to check out an area, leaving the rest of the family behind. They take whatever jobs they can to get by. Often their work is dangerous, and they face **discrimination** from English-speaking owners and workers.

In contrast, Canadians now come to the United States able to speak at least some English, even those from Quebec. They understand America's way of life because it is a lot like theirs. Many are educated **professionals** who can live and work wherever they please. A scientist can work for NASA in a big city such as Houston, Texas. A professor can teach at a college in a small town like Chapel Hill, North Carolina. There are no more "little Canadas."

That brings us back to the big question. If Canada is such a good place to live, why come to the United States at all?

Interesting Fact

▸ Canada's head of state is the reigning monarch of the United Kingdom. Queen Elizabeth II, who became queen in 1952, will hold this position until her death or until she steps down from the throne. Then her son, Charles, prince of Wales, will become king.

Of course, different people have different reasons. A college student may marry an American. A hockey player may play for a team in Chicago. But it's educated professionals who leave Canada the most—seven times more often than the average person. For these people, it comes down to two reasons—more money and better careers.

Wages in Canada are close to those in the United States. But many Canadian Americans dislike Canada's high taxes. Because of taxes, some people take home less money than workers doing the same job in the United States. Moving south of the border doesn't guarantee better pay. But the chance to make more money is hard to pass up.

Some professionals also want to work in the world's best hospitals and computer companies,

These students in Montreal may some day be faced with the decision of whether to stay in Canada or leave for the United States in the hopes of making more money and better opportunities.

often located in the United States. For example, Dr. Michelle Donato is a Canadian-born bone expert in Houston. She says she would prefer to live in Montreal, but her special kind of research is done only in the United States.

This is a common complaint. When asked, 48 percent of Canadian immigrants said the chance to work in the best facilities with the smartest people convinced them to leave Canada. Experts and ordinary Canadians continue to discuss how to deal with the problem.

Many of the world's best hospitals are located in the United States. Opportunities to work in facilities like this operating room at Johns Hopkins Hospital in Baltimore, Maryland, bring some of Canada's finest health professionals to the United States.

WHEN A COUNTRY'S EDUCATED WORKERS KEEP LEAVING TO LIVE SOMEWHERE else, it is called a brain drain. In the 1990s, thousands of educated workers from Canada flocked to the United States. Canadians wondered why. And soon they began to argue about the reasons.

Some blamed Canada's high taxes. Cut taxes, they said, and the professionals would stay. Otherwise, all the smartest people would leave the country.

Others disagreed. It's true Canadians paid higher taxes, they said. But not much more, and they got a lot for their money. They said professionals went to the United States because of better places to work. That had nothing to do with taxes. Besides, for every college graduate who left Canada, four more came to Canada from other countries. That was a "brain gain!"

There are other possible reasons. During the 1990s, Canada's government cut the number of people working in health care and colleges. Doctors, nurses, and teachers looked south for new jobs.

At the same time the American **high-tech** field was booming. For high-

tech scientists and computer experts, the United States offers the best laboratories in the world. Like everyone else, Canadians wanted to use the best tools. The North American Free Trade Agreement (NAFTA)—an agreement among the United States, Canada, and Mexico—made it easier for companies from each of the three countries to do business together. It also made it easier than ever for skilled workers from Canada and Mexico to work in the United States. Why not go?

And don't forget history. Ever since the Revolutionary War, Canadians have crossed the border looking for better lives. Perhaps this brain drain is just more of the same.

Chapter FOUR

Canadian-American Contributions

Interesting Fact

▶ Céline Dion is the youngest of 14 children. Her parents were both musicians. When she was five years old, she began performing with her brothers and sisters at a small club owned by her parents.

CANADIANS HAVE ADDED A LOT TO LIFE IN THE United States, especially when it comes to entertainment and sports.

California singer-songwriter Alanis Morrisette hails from Ottawa, Ontario. Singer Avril Lavigne now lives in New York City but grew up in Napanee, Ontario. Classic rocker Neil Young was born in Toronto and grew up in Winnipeg. And few entertainers are more popular than Céline Dion (born in Charlemagne, Quebec, and now living in Las Vegas), the rare singer who performs in both English and French.

It's hard to miss Canadian Americans on television or at the movies. Though not all are American citizens, most now live in California to be near Hollywood. Comedians Mike Myers and Jim Carrey were both born in Scarborough, Ontario. Superstar Keanu Reeves grew up in Toronto, which is also the birthplace of television news

26

anchor Peter Jennings. Vancouver has sent many actors south, including Michael J. Fox, Jason Priestley, and Josh Jackson.

Some Canadians might consider sports their greatest contribution to U.S. culture. The popularity of ice hockey soared in the United States when Canadian national hero Wayne Gretzky moved from Edmonton to Los Angeles. At one time, most National Hockey League teams played in cities near the Canadian border. Today, fans cheer on their favorite clubs in places like Tampa Bay, Dallas, and Phoenix.

Did you know that a Canadian invented basketball? Dr. James Naismith created the game in Massachusetts in 1891. He was born in Almonte, Ontario.

Entertainers and athletes are not the only Canadians to make their home in the United States. Scientist Richard Edward

Interesting Fact

▸ Canada's first national hockey organization was the Amateur Hockey Association. It was started in 1885 in the city of Montreal.

Wayne Gretzky is considered by many to be the best hockey player of all time. He led the Edmonton Oilers to four Stanley Cup Championships in the 1980s.

▶ Wayne Gretzky played 20 seasons in the National Hockey League and was inducted into the Hockey Hall of Fame in November 1999.

Taylor, born in Medicine Hat, Alberta, was one of the winners of the 1990 Nobel Prize in physics. Artist Agnes Martin was born in Macklin, Saskatchewan, and later moved to New Mexico. She is famous for her paintings and sculptures.

Canadian ideas and products, like kayaks and chocolate bars, cross the open border as easily as the people. Products and ideas from the United States cross the other way as well. Each country gains from the other. Yes, arguments pop up. But the special friendship between Canada and the United States still goes on after more than 100 years.

James Naismith, the inventor of the exciting sport of basketball was born in Almonte, Ontario. He invented the sport when he was given the task of creating an indoor game that would keep a rowdy class of boys busy through the long, cold, New England winter.

13,000 B.C. One of the earliest known human habitation sites in Canada, the Bluefish Caves, dates from this time.

A.D. 1534 Jacques Cartier reaches the St. Lawrence River and declares the land to be the property of France.

1605 Samuel de Champlain and Pierre du Mots found Port Royal, the first permanent European town in Canada; today, it is called Annapolis Royal.

1642 The city of Montreal is founded.

1673 Marquette and Joliet canoe south on the Mississippi River as far as present-day Arkansas.

1682 La Salle explores the Mississippi River as far as the Gulf of Mexico.

1702–1713 Queen Anne's War is fought between France and Great Britain.

1713 Great Britain takes control of Acadia and renames it Nova Scotia.

1754 The British expulsion of the French-speaking Acadians from Canada begins.

1785 Henri Peyroux de la Coudreniere leads 1,624 Acadians from France to new homes in Louisiana.

1850 French Canadians begin coming to New England to work in the logging industry.

1867 The Dominion of Canada is established, making the provinces of Ontario, Quebec, Nova Scotia, and New Brunswick part of an independent nation.

1880–1890 About 450,000 Canadians come to the United States.

1901 Oil is discovered in Louisiana.

1922 Louisiana's government bans the French language in public schools.

1930 Canadian immigration to the United States slows down as a result of the Great Depression.

1970 A new wave of Canadian immigrants begins to come to the United States.

1994 Canada, the United States, and Mexico sign the North American Free Trade Agreement (NAFTA).

ancestors (AN-sess-turz)
Ancestors are relatives from long ago. The Acadians of the 1700s are ancestors of the Cajuns living in Louisiana today.

bayou (BYE-oo)
A bayou is a creek or small river running through a swampy area. Louisiana's Cajuns learned how to live on the bayou.

culture (KUHL-chur)
A culture includes a people's language, ideas, customs, and way of life. Throughout the 20th century, Cajuns fought to preserve their culture.

discrimination (diss-krim-i-NAY-shuhn)
Discrimination is unfair treatment of a group of people based on their race, religion, country, culture, or other traits. New immigrants often face discrimination in the workplace.

environment (en-VYE-ruhn-muhnt)
The natural world, including the land, bodies of water, and air, is the environment. The oil industry damaged Louisiana's environment.

expulsion (ek-SPUL-shuhn)
An expulsion happens when one group forces another to leave a certain place. The expulsion of the Acadians from Nova Scotia began in 1754.

high-tech (HIGH-TECH)
Something that is high-tech uses the newest technology, especially in the fields of electronics and computers. For high-tech scientists and computer experts, the United States offers the best laboratories in the world.

immigrants (IM-uh-gruhnts)
Immigrants are people who leave their own country to make their home in another country. Canadian immigrants have been coming to the United States almost since the day the Revolutionary War ended.

patois (PA-twa)
A patois is a variation of a language that mixes foreign words and ideas with an already existing language. Cajuns use a patois that mixes French with words and ideas from English and other languages.

professionals (pruh-FESH-uh-nuhls)
Professionals are people who work in fields that require high levels of education, a long period of training, or both. Many Canadian professionals, such as doctors, nurses, and scientists, come to the United States to work.

province (PROV-uhnss)
A province is a region of a country that has its own government, but is also under the control of a larger, more powerful government. Some of Canada's provinces include Quebec, Ontario, and Nova Scotia.

For Further INFORMATION

Web Sites

Visit our homepage for lots of links about Canadian Americans:
http://www.childsworld.com/links.html

Note to Parents, Teachers, and Librarians:
We routinely verify our Web links to make sure they're safe,
active sites—so encourage your readers to check them out!

Books

Harmon, Daniel E. *La Salle and the Exploration of the Mississippi.* Philadelphia:
Chelsea House Publishers, 2001.

Hintz, Martin. *Louisiana.* Danbury, Conn.: Children's Press, 1998.

Parent, Michael, and Julien Olivier. *Of Kings and Fools: Stories of the French
Tradition in North America.* Little Rock, Ark.: August House, 1996.

Tallant, Robert. *Evangeline and the Acadians.* Gretna, La.: Pelican Publishing
Company, 2000.

Places to Visit or Contact

Acadian Museum
To learn more about the Acadians and their culture
203 South Broadway
Erath, LA 70533
337/937-5468

Illinois State Museum
*To learn more about Jacques Marquette and Louis Joliet and their exploration
of the Mississippi River*
Spring and Edwards Streets
Springfield, IL 62706-5000
217/782-7387

31

Index

About the Author

KEVIN CUNNINGHAM IS AN AUTHOR AND TRAVEL WRITER WHO has written for newspapers, magazines, and travel guides. He studied history and journalism at the University of Illinois at Urbana. When not writing he travels, plays cards, or tries to learn French. He lives in Chicago, Illinois.

Public Library
159 Main Street
Norfolk, MA 02056